WAS
MICHAEL JACKSON
FRAMED?

MARY A. FISCHER

ISBN 978-0-7867-5413-7

Cover Design: Sol Orena, DISFRAZDETIGRE /studio

PHOTO CREDITS
Cover by © GARY HERSHORN/Reuters/Corbis. Michael Jackson performing during halftime at the NFL's Super Bowl XXVII in Pasadena, Ca.
© Todd Gray 1981. MJ in Atlanta, Peachtree Hotel.
© Dorit Thies. Author photo
© Splash News. Evan Chandler
© Sam Mircovich/Reuters/Corbis. MJ representatives Pellicano and Fields
© Harrison Funk/ZUMA Press/Corbis. Anthony Pellicano and Howard Weitzman
© NICK UT/AP/Corbis - Michael Jackson, King of Pop

Distributed by Argo Navis Author Services

Distributed by
Argo Navis Author Services
www.argonavisdigital.com

ABOUT THE AUTHOR

Mary A. Fischer is a recipient of the John Bartlow Martin Award and has twice been a finalist for the National Magazine Award. For seven years, she was a senior writer at GQ and has contributed to The Atlantic, Men's Journal, Scotusblog, O Magazine, Rolling Stone and the Los Angeles Times. Several of her investigative articles have been produced as news magazine segments for Dateline, CNN, 48 Hours and ABC's Primetime. After her investigation of the 1993 Michael Jackson scandal generated national media attention and led to a re-examination of the case, she went on to investigate and write about other controversial, high-profile criminal cases. Fischer lives in Los Angeles.

FOREWORD

To this day, I continue to hear from people around the world asking about this story on the Michael Jackson case that I investigated and wrote for GQ magazine in 1994. Some want to know where they can get the article, which is one reason I'm publishing it now. The cover is new, and so are some of the photos, but the story is the original version I wrote in 1994.

Other people I hear from want to know how I came up with the idea for the story in the first place, and if I have any new details or updates about the key players in the case. Most of what I know has been widely reported. In November 2009, after years of grappling with his son Jordan's alleged molestation claims against Jackson, and being estranged from his son and facing a serious illness, Evan Chandler, 65, ended his pain with a gunshot to the head. The year before, Jackson's private investigator, Anthony Pellicano, was sentenced to 15 years in prison for running a wiretapping scheme that spied on the rich and famous. (In a 2011 exclusive interview http://goo.gl/fHg3L Pellicano broke his silence.) And a one-time Chandler family lawyer also went to prison for bankruptcy fraud.

Jordie Chander, now 33, admitted publicly in 2009 that he had lied about the allegations and that he was deeply sorry. But by then, four years after the second Jackson molestation case ended in a trial acquittal, it was too late to restore Jackson's public image.

Some people who make contact thank me for writing the story, which explored in depth the adults who first accused Jackson of sexually molesting Jordan Chandler. Amid the torrent of media coverage, it was, incredibly, a side of the story that had not yet been told. http://goo.gl/8dNBQ Way to go, some comment. It seems to be a story that people still want to hear.

All these years later, and now, two years after Michael Jackson's death, I am often reminded that the story's larger themes are still relevant today. In high-profile cases, the same rush to judgment by the media and public—us—that defined the Jackson case still permeates our culture. Exposed to unbridled press coverage that stresses sensationalism over substance, how can we ever expect to discover what the truth is? I've seen the damage done to people caught in the media's glare, when restraint, common sense and skepticism are abandoned in favor of unfounded speculation. We've lost something crucial to our system of justice and fairness—the presumption of innocence.

Now, to the question of how I got the idea for the GQ story.

It was Christmas, 1993, and I had rented a small cabin in the mountains near Los Angeles. It was snowing and I took my two dogs for a walk to the local market. In the newspaper kiosk I glanced at the front page story that said Michael Jackson had just been served with a warrant to strip search his body, as police wanted to verify Jordan Chandler's description of Jackson's private anatomy. I had been following the story since the beginning, when Evan Chandler first accused Jackson of sexually molesting his 13-year-old son.

But this latest development seemed absurd, and I couldn't get the case out of my mind. More and more it reminded me of another high-profile case that I had covered a few years before. The McMartin preschool child sex abuse case rocked the country with its bizarre allegations of ritualistic animal sacrifice, underground tunnels and molesting young children in airplanes and carwashes. All but one member of the McMartin family were arrested, along with several of the preschool's teachers, and the hysteria that swept through Southern California—and eventually the rest of the county—was palpable.

Most in the media bought into the prosecution's point of view that the McMartin defendants were monsters. Before any of them went on trial, the press and the public had convicted them. But certain things about the case didn't make sense to me and I began an investigation to try to get to the bottom of things. In time, based on evidence I found, I came to believe that the defendants had been falsely accused and the allegations against them were not credible.

In the end, two McMartin defendants—Ray Buckey and his mother, Peggy McMartin Buckey—went on trial and three years later, in what became the longest and costliest trial in U.S. history, both were acquitted, but not before they had lost everything, their life savings, their home, their reputations and the preschool, which was demolished and sold to a developer to pay attorneys' fees.

So, as I said, I couldn't stop thinking about the Jackson case. My experience of covering the McMartin case, and seeing how easily false accusations of child sexual abuse could be made to stick against an individual, especially one as famous as Michael Jackson, I went to the payphone outside the market and called my editor in New York.

I told him I thought there was more to the Jackson story. At that point, it was really only an educated hunch, a reporter's instinct that guided me. I didn't think I'd actually get the assignment because by then an avalanche of press from around the world had all but buried us with coverage. What else was there to tell? We had heard it all. Or had we?

I got the assignment and then sort of panicked. Where to start? Who would talk to me? How could I possibly find out any information that hadn't already been dug into by other reporters? Was I even on the right track?

I decided to investigate Jackson's main accusers—Evan Chandler and his attorney Barry Rothman–an angle the media had not yet explored in depth. I wanted to look closely at the people who first made the allegations and thus gain insight into their character and motives.

At first no one I called, none of the key players in the case, returned my calls. I called and left messages again. I wrote letters. Still no reponse. One afternoon I walked into Rent-A-Wreck, the car rental company owned by Jordie Chandler's step-father, Dave Schwartz, hoping an in-person interview request would convince him to talk to me. Sorry, Schwartz said, I've said everything I'm going to say.

Clearly, I was getting nowhere fast. What did I get myself into?

I switched gears and tried a different tack. I drove to "old faithful"— the records office in the basement of the criminal courthouse in downtown Los Angeles. I searched the computer for every case, civil or criminal, that had ever been filed by or against Jackson's accusers. Sometimes a reporter gets lucky and finds potential sources from aggrieved plaintiffs and defendants.

Up came gold. There were so many cases of former legal clients and other attorneys who had either sued or been sued by Barry Rothman, that I had to use a clerk's cart to wheel the stacks of files to the review table. In the files, I found all kinds of leads, and two, in particular, helped me break the case open. These sources cooperated on the condition that I not use their names or any other identifying information. We met in out-of-the way restaurants and they sent revealing documents to me in manila envelopes with no return address. Fearing that I might be recording our telephone conversations—I wasn't—one source never identified himself by name when I picked up the phone. He just started talking until I recognized his voice.

Another source, a lawyer connected to the Chandler family, had dodged my calls for weeks and then, one day, he finally agreed to meet. During our lunch, he wasn't telling me anything I didn't already know about Evan Chandler and his attorney, and then, just as I got ready to pay the check, he dropped the bombshell. Do you know about the drug given to Jordie, in a dentist's office, the lawyer casually asked? I hadn't known about it—the drug turned out to be sodium Amytal— and that piece of information, confirmed by a second knowledgeable source, eventually led to my uncovering the evidence I presented in the GQ story. No one from the defense side, other than private investigator Anthony Pellicano, ever talked to me. Not Michael Jackson, not his attorneys.

Today, given the sweeping changes in journalism and cutbacks in investigative reporting, I doubt whether either of these stories—McMartin or Michael Jackson—would see the light of day. Few media organizations today can afford to support the time it often takes to report investigative stories. That leaves me wondering, and worried, about the stories that need and deserve to be told, but aren't getting out because of cost.

Where does that leave us? On the second anniversary of Michael Jackson's death, it's clear his appeal continues to fascinate and flourish. Look at this http://vimeo.com/5545871 tribute for him. As for me, I continue to report stories, but still, all these years later, it is this GQ article and the one I wrote about the McMartin case in Los Angeles Magazine, that have had the biggest impact on the public—and on me.

Mary A. Fischer
June 2012

WAS MICHAEL JACKSON FRAMED?

Before O.J. Simpson, there was Michael Jackson—another beloved black celebrity seemingly brought down by allegations of scandal in his personal life. Those allegations—that Jackson had molested a 13-year-old boy—instigated a multimillion-dollar lawsuit, two grand-jury investigations and a shameless media circus. Jackson, in turn, filed charges of extortion against some of his accusers. Ultimately, the suit was settled out of court for a sum that has been estimated at $20 million; no criminal charges were brought against Jackson by the police or the grand juries. This past August, Jackson was in the news again, when Lisa Marie Presley, Elvis's daughter, announced that she and the singer had married.

As the dust settles on one of the nation's worst episodes of media excess, one thing is clear: The American public has never heard a defense of Michael Jackson. Until now.

It is, of course, impossible to prove a negative—that is, prove that something didn't happen. But it is possible to take an in-depth look at the people who made the allegations against Jackson and thus gain insight into their character and motives. What emerges from such an examination, based on court documents, business records and scores of interviews, is a persuasive argument that Jackson molested no one and that he himself may have been the victim of a well-conceived plan to extract money from him.

More than that, the story that arises from this previously unexplored territory is radically different from the tale that has been promoted by tabloid and even mainstream journalists. It is a story of greed, ambition, misconceptions on the part of police and prosecutors, a lazy and sensation-seeking media and the use of a powerful, hypnotic drug. It may also be a story about how a case was simply invented.

Neither Michael Jackson nor his current defense attorneys agreed to be interviewed for this article. Had they decided to fight the civil charges and go to trial, what follows might have served as the core of Jackson's defense—as well as the basis to further the extortion charges against his own accusers, which could well have exonerated the singer.

Jackson's troubles began when his van broke down on Wilshire Boulevard in Los Angeles in May 1992. Stranded in the middle of the heavily trafficked street, Jackson was spotted by the wife of Mel Green, an employee at Rent-a-Wreck, an offbeat car-rental agency a mile away. Green went to the rescue. When Dave Schwartz, the owner of the car-rental company, heard Green was bringing Jackson to the lot, he called his wife, June, and told her to come over with their 6-year-old daughter and her son from her previous marriage. The boy, then 12, was a big Jackson fan. Upon arriving, June Chandler Schwartz told Jackson about the time her son had sent him a drawing after the singer's hair caught on fire during the filming of a Pepsi commercial. Then she gave Jackson their home number.

Certain facts about the relationship are not in dispute. Jackson began calling the boy, and a friendship developed. After Jackson returned from a promotional tour, three months later, June Chandler Schwartz and her son and daughter became regular guests at Neverland, Jackson's ranch in Santa Barbara County. During the following year, Jackson showered the boy and his family with attention and gifts, including video games, watches, an after-hours shopping spree at Toys "R" Us and trips around the world—from Las Vegas and Disney World to Monaco and Paris.

Jordie Chandler,
age 13

By March 1993, Jackson and the boy were together frequently and the sleepovers began. June Chandler Schwartz had also become close to Jackson "and liked him enormously," one friend says. "He was the kindest man she had ever met."

Jackson's personal eccentricities—from his attempts to remake his face through plastic surgery to his preference for the company of children—have been widely reported. And while it may be unusual for a 35-year-old man to have sleepovers with a 13-year-old child, the boy's mother and others close to Jackson never thought it odd. Jackson's behavior is better understood once it's put in the context of his own childhood.

"Contrary to what you might think, Michael's life hasn't been a walk in the park," one of his attorneys says. Jackson's childhood essentially stopped—and his unorthodox life began—when he was 5 years old and living in Gary, Indiana. Michael spent his youth in rehearsal studios, on stages performing before millions of strangers and sleeping

Summer 1981. Presidential Suite, Peach Tree Hotel, Atlanta, Ga. Michael takes a moment to reflect after performing benefit concert for the missing and murdered children of Atlanta.

in an endless string of hotel rooms. Except for his eight brothers and sisters, Jackson was surrounded by adults who pushed him relentlessly, particularly his father, Joe Jackson—a strict, unaffectionate man who reportedly beat his children.

Jackson's early experiences translated into a kind of arrested development, many say, and he became a child in a man's body. "He never had a childhood," says Bert Fields, a former attorney of Jackson's. "He is having one now. His buddies are 12-year-old kids. They have pillow fights and food fights." Jackson's interest in children also translated into humanitarian efforts. Over the years, he has given millions to causes benefiting children, including his own Heal The World Foundation.

But there is another context—the one having to do with the times in which we live—in which most observers would evaluate Jackson's behavior. "Given the current confusion and hysteria over child sexual abuse," says Dr. Phillip Resnick, a noted Cleveland psychiatrist, "any

Evan Chandler

physical or nurturing contact with a child may be seen as suspicious, and the adult could well be accused of sexual misconduct."

GREAT EXPECTATIONS

Jackson's involvement with the boy was welcomed, at first, by all the adults in the youth's life—his mother, his stepfather and even his biological father, Evan Chandler (who also declined to be interviewed for this article). Born Evan Robert Charmatz in the Bronx in 1944, Chandler had reluctantly followed in the footsteps of his father and brothers and become a dentist. "He hated being a dentist," a family friend says. "He always wanted to be a writer." After moving in 1973 to West Palm Beach to practice dentistry, he changed his last name, believing Charmatz was "too Jewish-sounding," says a former colleague. Hoping somehow to become a screenwriter, Chandler moved to Los Angeles in the late Seventies with his wife, June Wong, an attractive Eurasian who had worked briefly as a model.

Chandler's dental career had its precarious moments. In December 1978, while working at the Crenshaw Family Dental Center, a clinic in a low-income area of L.A., Chandler did restoration work on sixteen of a patient's teeth during a single visit. An examination of the work,

5

the Board of Dental Examiners concluded, revealed "gross ignorance and/or inefficiency" in his profession. The board revoked his license; however, the revocation was stayed, and the board instead suspended him for ninety days and placed him on probation for two and a half years. Devastated, Chandler left town for New York. He wrote a film script but couldn't sell it.

Months later, Chandler returned to L.A. with his wife and held a series of dentistry jobs. By 1980, when their son was born, the couple's marriage was in trouble. "One of the reasons June left Evan was because of his temper," a family friend says. They divorced in 1985. The court awarded sole custody of the boy to his mother and ordered Chandler to pay $500 a month in child support, but a review of documents reveals that in 1993, when the Jackson scandal broke, Chandler owed his ex-wife $68,000—a debt she ultimately forgave.

A year before Jackson came into his son's life, Chandler had a second serious professional problem. One of his patients, a model, sued him for dental negligence after he did restoration work on some of her teeth. Chandler claimed that the woman had signed a consent form in which she'd acknowledged the risks involved. But when Edwin Zinman, her attorney, asked to see the original records, Chandler said they had been stolen from the trunk of his Jaguar. He provided a duplicate set. Zinman, suspicious, was unable to verify the authenticity of the records. "What an extraordinary coincidence that they were stolen," Zinman says now. "That's like saying 'The dog ate my homework.' " The suit was eventually settled out of court for an undisclosed sum.

Despite such setbacks, Chandler by then had a successful practice in Beverly Hills. And he got his first break in Hollywood in 1992, when he co-wrote the Mel Brooks film Robin Hood: Men in Tights. Until Michael Jackson entered his son's life, Chandler hadn't shown all that much interest in the boy. "He kept promising to buy him a computer so they could work on scripts together, but he never did," says Michael Freeman, formerly an attorney for June Chandler Schwartz. Chandler's dental practice kept him busy, and he had started a new family by then, with two small children by his second wife, a corporate attorney.

At first, Chandler welcomed and encouraged his son's relationship with Michael Jackson, bragging about it to friends and associates. When Jackson and the boy stayed with Chandler during May 1993, Chandler urged the entertainer to spend more time with his son at his house. According to sources, Chandler even suggested that Jackson build an addition onto the house so the singer could stay there. After calling the zoning department and discovering it couldn't be done, Chandler made another suggestion—that Jackson just build him a new home.

That same month, the boy, his mother and Jackson flew to Monaco for the World Music Awards. "Evan began to get jealous of the involvement and felt left out," Freeman says. Upon their return, Jackson and the boy again stayed with Chandler, which pleased him—a five-day visit, during which they slept in a room with the youth's half brother. Though Chandler has admitted that Jackson and the boy always had their clothes on whenever he saw them in bed together, he claimed that it was during this time that his suspicions of sexual misconduct were triggered. At no time has Chandler claimed to have witnessed any sexual misconduct on Jackson's part.

THE SECRET PHONE CALL

Chandler became increasingly volatile, making threats that alienated Jackson, Dave Schwartz and June Chandler Schwartz. In early July 1993, Dave Schwartz, who had been friendly with Chandler, secretly tape-recorded a lengthy telephone conversation he had with him. During the conversation, Chandler talked of his concern for his son and his anger at Jackson and at his ex-wife, whom he described as "cold and heartless." When Chandler tried to "get her attention" to discuss his suspicions about Jackson, he says on the tape, she told him "Go fuck yourself."

"I had a good communication with Michael," Chandler told Schwartz. "We were friends. I liked him and I respected him and everything else for what he is. There was no reason why he had to stop

Dave Schwartz

calling me. I sat in the room one day and talked to Michael and told him exactly what I want out of this whole relationship. What I want."

Admitting to Schwartz that he had "been rehearsed" about what to say and what not to say, Chandler never mentioned money during their conversation. When Schwartz asked what Jackson had done that made Chandler so upset, Chandler alleged only that "he broke up the family. [The boy] has been seduced by this guy's power and money." Both men repeatedly berated themselves as poor fathers to the boy.

Elsewhere on the tape, Chandler indicated he was prepared to move against Jackson: "It's already set," Chandler told Schwartz. "There are other people involved that are waiting for my phone call that are in certain positions. I've paid them to do it. Everything's going according to a certain plan that isn't just mine. Once I make that phone call, this guy [his attorney, Barry K. Rothman, presumably] is going to destroy everybody in sight in any devious, nasty, cruel way that he can do it. And I've given him full authority to do that."

Chandler then predicted what would, in fact, transpire six weeks later: "And if I go through with this, I win big-time. There's no way I lose. I've checked that inside out. I will get everything I want, and they will be destroyed forever. June will lose [custody of the son]...and Michael's career will be over."

"Does that help [the boy]?" Schwartz asked.

"That's irrelevant to me," Chandler replied. "It's going to be bigger than all of us put together. The whole thing is going to crash down on everybody and destroy everybody in sight. It will be a massacre if I don't get what I want."

Instead of going to the police, seemingly the most appropriate action in a situation involving suspected child molestation, Chandler had turned to a lawyer. And not just any lawyer. He'd turned to Barry Rothman.

A LAWYER'S SECRETS

"This attorney I found, I picked the nastiest son of a bitch I could find," Chandler said in the recorded conversation with Schwartz. "All he wants to do is get this out in the public as fast as he can, as big as he can, and humiliate as many people as he can. He's nasty, he's mean, he's very smart, and he's hungry for the publicity." (Through his attorney, Wylie Aitken, Rothman declined to be interviewed for this article. Aitken agreed to answer general questions limited to the Jackson case, and then only about aspects that did not involve Chandler or the boy.)

To know Rothman, says a former colleague who worked with him during the Jackson case, and who kept a diary of what Rothman and Chandler said and did in Rothman's office, is to believe that Barry could have "devised this whole plan, period. This [making allegations against Michael Jackson] is within the boundary of his character, to do something like this." Information supplied by Rothman's former clients, associates and employees reveals a pattern of manipulation and deceit.

Rothman has a general-law practice in Century City. At one time, he negotiated music and concert deals for Little Richard, the Rolling Stones, the Who, ELO and Ozzy Osbourne. Gold and platinum records commemorating those days still hang on the walls of his office. With his grayish-white beard and perpetual tan—which he maintains in a tanning bed at his house—Rothman reminds a former client of "a

9

leprechaun." To a former employee, Rothman is "a demon" with "a terrible temper." His most cherished possession, acquaintances say, is his 1977 Rolls-Royce Corniche, which carries the license plate "BKR 1." Over the years, Rothman has made so many enemies that his ex-wife once expressed, to her attorney, surprise that someone "hadn't done him in." He has a reputation for stiffing people. "He appears to be a professional deadbeat... He pays almost no one," investigator Ed Marcus concluded (in a report filed in Los Angeles Superior Court, as part of a lawsuit against Rothman), after reviewing the attorney's credit profile, which listed more than thirty creditors and judgment holders who were chasing him. In addition, more than twenty civil lawsuits involving Rothman have been filed in Superior Court, several complaints have been made to the Labor Commission and disciplinary actions for three incidents have been taken against him by the state bar of California. In 1992, he was suspended for a year, though that suspension was stayed and he was instead placed on probation for the term.

In 1987, Rothman was $16,800 behind in alimony and child-support payments. Through her attorney, his ex-wife, Joanne Ward, threatened to attach Rothman's assets, but he agreed to make good on the debt. A year later, after Rothman still hadn't made the payments, Ward's attorney tried to put a lien on Rothman's expensive Sherman Oaks home. To their surprise, Rothman said he no longer owned the house; three years earlier, he'd deeded the property to Tinoa Operations, Inc., a Panamanian shell corporation. According to Ward's lawyer, Rothman claimed that he'd had $200,000 of Tinoa's money, in cash, at his house one night when he was robbed at gunpoint. The only way he could make good on the loss was to deed his home to Tinoa, he told them. Ward and her attorney suspected the whole scenario was a ruse, but they could never prove it. It was only after sheriff's deputies had towed away Rothman's Rolls Royce that he began paying what he owed. Documents filed with Los Angeles Superior Court seem to confirm the suspicions of Ward and her attorney. These show that Rothman created an elaborate network of foreign bank accounts and shell companies, seemingly to conceal some of his assets—in particular, his home and much of the $531,000 proceeds from its eventual sale, in 1989. The companies, including Tinoa, can be traced to Rothman. He bought a Panamanian shelf company (an existing but non-operating firm) and arranged matters so that though his name would not appear on the list of its officers, he would have unconditional power of attorney, in effect leaving him in control of moving money in and out.

Meanwhile, Rothman's employees didn't fare much better than his ex-wife. Former employees say they sometimes had to beg for their paychecks. And sometimes the checks that they did get would bounce. He couldn't keep legal secretaries. "He'd demean and humiliate them," says one. Temporary workers fared the worst. "He would work them for two weeks," adds the legal secretary, "then run them off by yelling at them and saying they were stupid. Then he'd tell the agency he was dissatisfied with the temp and wouldn't pay." Some agencies finally got wise and made Rothman pay cash up front before they'd do business with him.

The state bar's 1992 disciplining of Rothman grew out of a conflict-of-interest matter. A year earlier, Rothman had been kicked off a case by a client, Muriel Metcalf, whom he'd been representing in child-support and custody proceedings; Metcalf later accused him of padding her bill. Four months after Metcalf fired him, Rothman, without notifying her, began representing the company of her estranged companion, Bob Brutzman.

The case is revealing for another reason: It shows that Rothman had some experience dealing with child-molestation allegations before the Jackson scandal. Metcalf, while Rothman was still representing her, had accused Brutzman of molesting their child (which Brutzman denied). Rothman's knowledge of Metcalf's charges didn't prevent him from going to work for Brutzman's company—a move for which he was disciplined.

By 1992, Rothman was running from numerous creditors. Folb Management, a corporate real-estate agency, was one. Rothman owed the company $53,000 in back rent and interest for an office on Sunset Boulevard. Folb sued. Rothman then countersued, claiming that the building's security was so inadequate that burglars were able to steal more than $6,900 worth of equipment from his office one night. In the course of the proceedings, Folb's lawyer told the court, "Mr. Rothman is not the kind of person whose word can be taken at face value."

In November 1992, Rothman had his law firm file for bankruptcy, listing thirteen creditors—including Folb Management—with debts totaling $880,000 and no acknowledged assets. After reviewing the bankruptcy papers, an ex-client whom Rothman was suing for $400,000 in legal fees noticed that Rothman had failed to list a $133,000 asset. The former client threatened to expose Rothman for "defrauding his creditors"—a felony—if he didn't drop the lawsuit. Cornered, Rothman had the suit dismissed in a matter of hours.

Six months before filing for bankruptcy, Rothman had transferred title on his Rolls-Royce to Majo, a fictitious company he controlled. Three years earlier, Rothman had claimed a different corporate owner for the car—Longridge Estates, a subsidiary of Tinoa Operations, the company that held the deed to his home. On corporation papers filed by Rothman, the addresses listed for Longridge and Tinoa were the same, 1554 Cahuenga Boulevard—which, as it turns out, is that of a Chinese restaurant in Hollywood.

It was with this man, in June 1993, that Evan Chandler began carrying out the "certain plan" to which he referred in his taped conversation with Dave Schwartz. At a graduation that month, Chandler confronted his ex-wife with his suspicions. "She thought the whole thing was baloney," says her ex-attorney, Michael Freeman. She told Chandler that she planned to take their son out of school in the fall so they could accompany Jackson on his "Dangerous" world tour. Chandler became irate and, say several sources, threatened to go public with the evidence he claimed he had on Jackson. "What parent in his right mind would want to drag his child into the public spotlight?" asks Freeman. "If something like this actually occurred, you'd want to protect your child."

PI Anthony Pellicano and attorney Bert Fields

Jackson asked his then-lawyer, Bert Fields, to intervene. One of the most prominent attorneys in the entertainment industry, Fields has been representing Jackson since 1990 and had negotiated for him, with Sony, the biggest music deal ever—with possible earnings of $700 million. Fields brought in investigator Anthony Pellicano to help sort things out. Pellicano does things Sicilian-style, being fiercely loyal to those he likes but a ruthless hardball player when it comes to his enemies.

On July 9, 1993, Dave Schwartz and June Chandler Schwartz played the taped conversation for Pellicano. "After listening to the tape for ten minutes, I knew it was about extortion," says Pellicano. That same day, he drove to Jackson's Century City condominium, where Chandler's son and the boy's half-sister were visiting. Without Jackson there, Pellicano "made eye contact" with the boy and asked him, he says, "very pointed questions": "Has Michael ever touched you? Have you ever seen him naked in bed?" The answer to all the questions was no. The boy repeatedly denied that anything bad had happened. On July 11, after Jackson had declined to meet with Chandler, the boy's father and Rothman went ahead with another part of the plan—they needed to get custody of the boy. Chandler asked his ex-wife to let the youth stay with him for a "one-week visitation period." As Bert Fields later said in an affidavit to the court, June Chandler Schwartz allowed the boy to go based on Rothman's assurance to Fields that her son would come back to her after the specified time, never guessing that Rothman's word would be worthless and that Chandler would not return their son.

Wylie Aitken, Rothman's attorney, claims that "at the time [Rothman] gave his word, it was his intention to have the boy returned." However, once "he learned that the boy would be whisked out of the country [to go on tour with Jackson], I don't think Mr. Rothman had any other choice." But the chronology clearly indicates that Chandler had learned in June, at the graduation, that the boy's mother planned to take her son on the tour. The taped telephone conversation made in early July, before Chandler took custody of his son, also seems to verify that Chandler and Rothman had no intention of abiding by the visitation agreement. "They [the boy and his mother] don't know it yet," Chandler told Schwartz, "but they aren't going anywhere." On July 12, one day after Chandler took control of his son, he had his ex-wife sign a document prepared by Rothman that prevented her from taking the youth out of Los Angeles County. This meant the boy would be unable to accompany Jackson on the tour. His mother told the court she signed the document under duress. Chandler, she said in an affidavit, had threatened that "I would not have [the boy] returned to me." A bitter custody battle ensued, making even murkier any charges Chandler made about wrongdoing on Jackson's part. (As of this August [1994], the boy was still living with Chandler.) It was during the first few weeks after Chandler took control of his son—who was now isolated from his friends, mother and stepfather—that the boy's allegations began to take shape.

At the same time, Rothman, seeking an expert's opinion to help establish the allegations against Jackson, called Dr. Mathis Abrams, a Beverly Hills psychiatrist. Over the telephone, Rothman presented Abrams with a hypothetical situation. In reply and without having met either Chandler or his son, Abrams on July 15 sent Rothman a two-page letter in which he stated that "reasonable suspicion would exist that sexual abuse may have occurred." Importantly, he also stated that if this were a real and not a hypothetical case, he would be required by law to report the matter to the Los Angeles County Department of Children's Services (DCS).

According to a July 27 entry in the diary kept by Rothman's former colleague, it's clear that Rothman was guiding Chandler in the plan. "Rothman wrote letter to Chandler advising him how to report child abuse without liability to parent," the entry reads.

At this point, there still had been made no demands or formal accusations, only veiled assertions that had become intertwined with a fierce custody battle. On August 4, 1993, however, things became very clear. Chandler and his son met with Jackson and Pellicano in a suite at the Westwood Marquis Hotel. On seeing Jackson, says Pellicano, Chandler gave the singer an affectionate hug (a gesture, some say, that would seem to belie the dentist's suspicions that Jackson had molested his son), then reached into his pocket, pulled out Abrams's letter and began reading passages from it. When Chandler got to the parts about child molestation, the boy, says Pellicano, put his head down and then looked up at Jackson with a surprised expression, as if to say "I didn't say that." As the meeting broke up, Chandler pointed his finger at Jackson, says Pellicano, and warned "I'm going to ruin you."

At a meeting with Pellicano in Rothman's office later that evening, Chandler and Rothman made their demand–$20 million.

On August 13, there was another meeting in Rothman's office. Pellicano came back with a counteroffer—a $350,000 screenwriting deal. Pellicano says he made the offer as a way to resolve the custody dispute and give Chandler an opportunity to spend more time with his son by working on a screenplay together. Chandler rejected the offer. Rothman made a counter-demand—a deal for three screenplays or nothing—which was spurned. In the diary of Rothman's ex-colleague, an August 24 entry reveals Chandler's disappointment: "I almost had a $20 million deal," he was overheard telling Rothman.

A DAY AT THE DENTIST

Before Chandler took control of his son, the only one making allegations against Jackson was Chandler himself—the boy had never accused the singer of any wrongdoing. That changed one day in Chandler's Beverly Hills dental office.

In the presence of Chandler and Mark Torbiner, a dental anesthesiologist, the boy was administered the controversial drug sodium Amytal—which some mistakenly believe is a truth serum. And it was after this session that the boy first made his charges against Jackson. A newsman at KCBS-TV, in L.A., reported on May 3 of this year that Chandler had used the drug on his son, but the dentist claimed he did so only to pull his son's tooth and that while under the drug's influence, the boy came out with allegations. Asked for this article about his use of the drug on the boy, Torbiner replied: "If I used it, it was for dental purposes."

Given the facts about sodium Amytal and a recent landmark case that involved the drug, the boy's allegations, say several medical experts, must be viewed as unreliable, if not highly questionable.

"It's a psychiatric medication that cannot be relied on to produce fact," says Dr. Phillip Resnick, a noted Cleveland psychiatrist. "People are very suggestible under it. People will say things under sodium Amytal that are blatantly untrue." Sodium Amytal is a barbiturate, an invasive drug that puts people in a hypnotic state when it's injected intravenously. Primarily administered for the treatment of amnesia, it first came into use during World War II, on soldiers traumatized—some into catatonic states—by the horrors of war. Scientific studies done in 1952 debunked the drug as a truth serum and instead demonstrated its risks: False memories can be easily implanted in those under its influence. "It is quite possible to implant an idea through the mere asking of a question," says Resnick. But its effects are apparently even more insidious: "The idea can become their memory, and studies have shown that even when you tell them the truth, they will swear on a stack of Bibles that it happened," he adds.

Recently, the reliability of the drug became an issue in a high-profile trial in Napa County, California. After undergoing numerous therapy sessions, at least one of which included the use of sodium Amytal, 20-year-old Holly Ramona accused her father of molesting her as a child. Gary Ramona vehemently denied the charge and sued his daughter's therapist and the psychiatrist who had administered the drug. This past May, jurors sided with Gary Ramona, believing that the therapist and the psychiatrist may have reinforced memories that were false. Gary Ramona's was the first successful legal challenge to the so-called "repressed memory phenomenon" that has produced thousands of sexual-abuse allegations over the past decade.

As for Chandler's story about using the drug to sedate his son during a tooth extraction, that too seems dubious, in light of the drug's customary use. "It's absolutely a psychiatric drug," says Dr. Kenneth Gottlieb, a San Francisco psychiatrist who has administered sodium Amytal to amnesia patients. Dr. John Yagiela, the coordinator of the anesthesia and pain control department of UCLA's school of dentistry, adds, "It's unusual for it to be used [for pulling a tooth]. It makes no sense when better, safer alternatives are available. It would not be my choice."

Because of sodium Amytal's potential side effects, some doctors will administer it only in a hospital. "I would never want to use a drug that tampers with a person's unconscious unless there was no other drug available," says Gottlieb. "And I would not use it without resuscitating equipment, in case of allergic reaction, and only with an M.D. anesthesiologist present."

Chandler, it seems, did not follow these guidelines. He had the procedure performed on his son in his office, and he relied on the dental anesthesiologist Mark Torbiner for expertise. (It was Torbiner who'd introduced Chandler and Rothman in 1991, when Rothman needed dental work.)

The nature of Torbiner's practice appears to have made it highly successful. "He boasts that he has $100 a month overhead and $40,000 a month income," says Nylla Jones, a former patient of his. Torbiner doesn't have an office for seeing patients; rather, he travels to various dental offices around the city, where he administers anesthesia during procedures.

This magazine has learned that the U.S. Drug Enforcement Administration is probing another aspect of Torbiner's business practices: He makes house calls to administer drugs—mostly morphine and Demerol—not only postoperatively to his dental patients but also, it seems, to those suffering pain whose source has nothing to do with dental work. He arrives at the homes of his clients—some of them celebrities—carrying a kind of fishing-tackle box that contains drugs and syringes. At one time, the license plate on his Jaguar read "SLPY-DOC." According to Jones, Torbiner charges $350 for a basic ten-to-twenty-minute visit. In what Jones describes as standard practice, when it's unclear how long Torbiner will need to stay, the client, anticipating the stupor that will soon set in, leaves a blank check for Torbiner to fill in with the appropriate amount.

Torbiner wasn't always successful. In 1989, he got caught in a lie and was asked to resign from UCLA, where he was an assistant professor at the school of dentistry. Torbiner had asked to take a half-day off so he could observe a religious holiday but was later found to have worked at a dental office instead.

A check of Torbiner's credentials with the Board of Dental Examiners indicates that he is restricted by law to administering drugs solely for dental-related procedures. But there is clear evidence that he has not abided by those restrictions. In fact, on at least eight occasions, Torbiner has given a general anesthetic to Barry Rothman, during hair-transplant procedures. Though normally a local anesthetic would be injected into the scalp, "Barry is so afraid of the pain," says Dr. James De Yarman, the San Diego physician who performed Rothman's transplants, "that [he] wanted to be put out completely." De Yarman said he was "amazed" to learn that Torbiner is a dentist, having assumed all along that he was an M.D.

In another instance, Torbiner came to the home of Nylla Jones, she says, and injected her with Demerol to help dull the pain that followed her appendectomy.

On August 16, three days after Chandler and Rothman rejected the $350,000 script deal, the situation came to a head. On behalf of June Chandler Schwartz, Michael Freeman notified Rothman that he would be filing papers early the next morning that would force Chandler to turn over the boy. Reacting quickly, Chandler took his son to Mathis Abrams, the psychiatrist who'd provided Rothman with his assessment of the hypothetical child-abuse situation. During a three-hour session, the boy alleged that Jackson had engaged in a sexual relationship with him. He talked of masturbation, kissing, fondling of nipples and oral sex. There was, however, no mention of actual penetration, which might have been verified by a medical exam, thus providing corroborating evidence.

The next step was inevitable. Abrams, who is required by law to report any such accusation to authorities, called a social worker at the Department of Children's Services, who in turn contacted the police. The full-scale investigation of Michael Jackson was about to begin.

Five days after Abrams called the authorities, the media got wind of the investigation. On Sunday morning, August 22, Don Ray, a freelance reporter in Burbank, was asleep when his phone rang. The caller, one of his tipsters, said that warrants had been issued to search Jackson's ranch and condominium. Ray sold the story to L.A.'s KNBC-TV, which broke the news at 4 P.M. the following day. After that, Ray "watched this story go away like a freight train," he says. Within twenty-four hours, Jackson was the lead story on seventy-three TV news broadcasts in the Los Angeles area alone and was on the front page of every British newspaper. The story of Michael Jackson and the 13-year-old boy became a frenzy of hype and unsubstantiated rumor, with the line between tabloid and mainstream media virtually eliminated.

The extent of the allegations against Jackson wasn't known until August 25. A person inside the DCS illegally leaked a copy of the abuse report to Diane Dimond of Hard Copy. Within hours, the L.A. office of a British news service also got the report and began selling copies to any reporter willing to pay $750. The following day, the world knew about the graphic details in the leaked report. "While laying next to each other in bed, Mr. Jackson put his hand under [the child's] shorts," the social worker had written. From there, the coverage soon demonstrated that anything about Jackson would be fair game.

"Competition among news organizations became so fierce," says KNBC reporter Conan Nolan, that "stories weren't being checked out. It was very unfortunate." The National Enquirer put twenty reporters and editors on the story. One team knocked on 500 doors in Brentwood trying to find Evan Chandler and his son. Using property records, they finally did, catching up with Chandler in his black Mercedes. "He was not a happy man. But I was," said Andy O'Brien, a tabloid photographer.

NEXT CAME THE ACCUSERS

Jackson's former employees. First, Stella and Philippe Lemarque, Jackson' ex-housekeepers, tried to sell their story to the tabloids with the help of broker Paul Barresi, a former porn star. They asked for as much as half a million dollars but wound up selling an interview to The Globe of Britain for $15,000. The Quindoys, a Filipino couple who had worked at Neverland, followed. When their asking price was $100,000, they said, " 'the hand was outside the kid's pants,' " Barresi told a producer of Frontline, a PBS program. "As soon as their price went up to $500,000, the hand went inside the pants. So come on." The L.A. district attorney's office eventually concluded that both couples were useless as witnesses.

Next came the bodyguards. Purporting to take the journalistic high road, Hard Copy's Diane Dimond told Frontline in early November of last year that her program was "pristinely clean on this. We paid no money for this story at all." But two weeks later, as a Hard Copy contract reveals, the show was negotiating a $100,000 payment to five former Jackson security guards who were planning to file a $10 million lawsuit alleging wrongful termination of their jobs.

On December 1, with the deal in place, two of the guards appeared on the program; they had been fired, Dimond told viewers, because "they knew too much about Michael Jackson's strange relationship with young boys." In reality, as their depositions under oath three months later reveal, it was clear they had never actually seen Jackson do anything improper with Chandler's son or any other child:

"So you don't know anything about Mr. Jackson and [the boy], do you?" one of Jackson's attorneys asked former security guard Morris Williams under oath.

"All I know is from the sworn documents that other people have sworn to."

"But other than what someone else may have said, you have no firsthand knowledge about Mr. Jackson and [the boy], do you?"

"That's correct."

"Have you spoken to a child who has ever told you that Mr. Jackson did anything improper with the child?"

"No."

When asked by Jackson's attorney where he had gotten his impressions, Williams replied: "Just what I've been hearing in the media and what I've experienced with my own eyes."

"Okay. That's the point. You experienced nothing with your own eyes, did you?"

"That's right, nothing."

(The guards' lawsuit, filed in March 1994, was still pending as this article went to press.)

[NOTE: The case was thrown out of court in July 1995.]

Next came the maid. On December 15, Hard Copy presented "The Bedroom Maid's Painful Secret." Blanca Francia told Dimond and other reporters that she had seen a naked Jackson taking showers and Jacuzzi baths with young boys. She also told Dimond that she had witnessed her own son in compromising positions with Jackson—an allegation that the grand juries apparently never found credible.

A copy of Francia's sworn testimony reveals that Hard Copy paid her $20,000, and had Dimond checked out the woman's claims, she would have found them to be false. Under deposition by a Jackson attorney, Francia admitted she had never actually see Jackson shower with anyone nor had she seen him naked with boys in his Jacuzzi. They always had their swimming trunks on, she acknowledged.

The coverage, says Michael Levine, a Jackson press representative, "followed a proctologist's view of the world. Hard Copy was loathsome. The vicious and vile treatment of this man in the media was for selfish reasons. [Even] if you have never bought a Michael Jackson record in your life, you should be very concerned. Society is built on very few pillars. One of them is truth. When you abandon that, it's a slippery slope."

The investigation of Jackson, which by October 1993 would grow to involve at least twelve detectives from Santa Barbara and Los Angeles counties, was instigated in part by the perceptions of one psychiatrist, Mathis Abrams, who had no particular expertise in child sexual abuse. Abrams, the DCS caseworker's report noted, "feels the child is telling the truth." In an era of widespread and often false claims of child molestation, police and prosecutors have come to give great weight to the testimony of psychiatrists, therapists and social workers.

Police seized Jackson's telephone books during the raid on his residences in August and questioned close to thirty children and their families. Some, such as Brett Barnes and Wade Robson, said they had shared Jackson's bed, but like all the others, they gave the same response—Jackson had done nothing wrong. "The evidence was very good for us," says an attorney who worked on Jackson's defense. "The other side had nothing but a big mouth."

Despite the scant evidence supporting their belief that Jackson was guilty, the police stepped up their efforts. Two officers flew to the Philippines to try to nail down the Quindoys' "hand in the pants" story, but apparently decided it lacked credibility. The police also employed aggressive investigative techniques—including allegedly telling lies—to push the children into making accusations against Jackson. According to several parents who complained to Bert Fields, officers told them unequivocally that their children had been molested, even though the children denied to their parents that anything bad had happened. The police, Fields complained in a letter to Los Angeles

Police Chief Willie Williams, "have also frightened youngsters with outrageous lies, such as 'We have nude photos of you.' There are, of course, no such photos." One officer, Federico Sicard, told attorney Michael Freeman that he had lied to the children he'd interviewed and told them that he himself had been molested as a child, says Freeman. Sicard did not respond to requests for an interview for this article.

All along, June Chandler Schwartz rejected the charges Chandler was making against Jackson—until a meeting with police in late August 1993. Officers Sicard and Rosibel Ferrufino made a statement that began to change her mind. "[The officers] admitted they only had one boy," says Freeman, who attended the meeting, "but they said, 'We're convinced Michael Jackson molested this boy because he fits the classic profile of a pedophile perfectly.' "

"There's no such thing as a classic profile. They made a completely foolish and illogical error," says Dr. Ralph Underwager, a Minneapolis psychiatrist who has treated pedophiles and victims of incest since 1953. Jackson, he believes, "got nailed" because of "misconceptions like these that have been allowed to parade as fact in an era of hysteria." In truth, as a U.S. Department of Health and Human Services study shows, many child-abuse allegations—48 percent of those filed in 1990—proved to be unfounded.

"It was just a matter of time before someone like Jackson became a target," says psychiatrist Phillip Resnick. "He's rich, bizarre, hangs around with kids and there is a fragility to him. The atmosphere is such that an accusation must mean it happened."

The seeds of settlement were already being sown as the police investigation continued in both counties through the fall of 1993. And a behind-the-scenes battle among Jackson's lawyers for control of the case, which would ultimately alter the course the defense would take, had begun.

By then, June Chandler Schwartz and Dave Schwartz had united with Evan Chandler against Jackson. The boy's mother, say several sources, feared what Chandler and Rothman might do if she didn't side with them. She worried that they would try to advance a charge against her of parental neglect for allowing her son to have sleepovers with Jackson. Her attorney, Michael Freeman, in turn, resigned in disgust, saying later that "the whole thing was such a mess. I felt uncomfortable with Evan. He isn't a genuine person, and I sensed he wasn't playing things straight."

Over the months, lawyers for both sides were retained, demoted and ousted as they feuded over the best strategy to take. Rothman ceased being Chandler's lawyer in late August, when the Jackson camp filed extortion charges against the two. Both then hired high-priced criminal defense attorneys to represent them. (Rothman retained Robert Shapiro, now O.J. Simpson's chief lawyer.) According to the diary kept by Rothman's former colleague, on August 26, before the extortion charges were filed, Chandler was heard to say, "It's my ass that's on the line and in danger of going to prison." The investigation into the extortion charges was superficial because, says a source, "the police never took it that seriously. But a whole lot more could have been done." For example, as they had done with Jackson, the police could have sought warrants to search the homes and offices of Rothman and Chandler. And when both men, through their attorneys, declined to be interviewed by police, a grand jury could have been convened.

"It was just a matter of time before someone like Jackson became a target. He's rich, bizarre [and] hangs around with kids."

In mid-September, Larry Feldman, a civil attorney who'd served as head of the Los Angeles Trial Lawyers Association, began representing Chandler's son and immediately took control of the situation. He filed a $30 million civil lawsuit against Jackson, which would prove to be the beginning of the end.

Once news of the suit spread, the wolves began lining up at the door. According to a member of Jackson's legal team, "Feldman got dozens of letters from all kinds of people saying they'd been molested by Jackson. They went through all of them trying to find somebody, and they found zero."

Anthony Pellicano and attorney Howard Weitzman

With the possibility of criminal charges against Jackson now loom-
ing, Bert Fields brought in Howard Weitzman, a well-known criminal-
defense lawyer with a string of high-profile clients—including John
DeLorean, whose trail he won, and Kim Basinger, whose Boxing
Helena contract dispute he lost. (Also, for a short time this June,
Weitzman was O.J. Simpson's attorney.) Some predicted a problem
between the two lawyers early on. There wasn't room for two strong
attorneys used to running their own show.

From the day Weitzman joined Jackson's defense team, "he was
talking settlement," says Bonnie Ezkenazi, an attorney who worked
for the defense. With Fields and Pellicano still in control of Jackson's
defense, they adopted an aggressive strategy. They believed staunchly
in Jackson's innocence and vowed to fight the charges in court. Pellicano began gathering evidence to use in the trial, which was scheduled
for March 21, 1994. "They had a very weak case," says Fields. "We
wanted to fight. Michael wanted to fight and go through a trial. We
felt we could win."

Dissension within the Jackson camp accelerated on November 12, after Jackson's publicist announced at a press conference that the singer was canceling the remainder of his world tour to go into a drug-rehabilitation program to treat his addiction to painkillers. Fields later told reporters that Jackson was "barely able to function adequately on an intellectual level." Others in Jackson's camp felt it was a mistake to portray the singer as incompetent. "It was important," Fields says, "to tell the truth. [Larry] Feldman and the press took the position that Michael was trying to hide and that it was all a scam. But it wasn't."

On November 23, the friction peaked. Based on information he says he got from Weitzman, Fields told a courtroom full of reporters that a criminal indictment against Jackson seemed imminent. Fields had a reason for making the statement: He was trying to delay the boy's civil suit by establishing that there was an impending criminal case that should be tried first. Outside the courtroom, reporters asked why Fields had made the announcement, to which Weitzman replied essentially that Fields "misspoke himself." The comment infuriated Fields, "because it wasn't true," he says. "It was just an outrage. I was very upset with Howard." Fields sent a letter of resignation to Jackson the following week.

"There was this vast group of people all wanting to do a different thing, and it was like moving through molasses to get a decision," says Fields. "It was a nightmare, and I wanted to get the hell out of it." Pellicano, who had received his share of flak for his aggressive manner, resigned at the same time.

With Fields and Pellicano gone, Weitzman brought in Johnnie Cochran Jr., a well-known civil attorney who is now helping defend O.J. Simpson. And John Branca, whom Fields had replaced as Jackson's general counsel in 1990, was back on board. In late 1993, as DAs in both Santa Barbara and Los Angeles counties convened grand juries to assess whether criminal charges should be filed against Jackson, the defense strategy changed course and talk of settling the civil case began in earnest, even though his new team also believed in Jackson's innocence.

A KEY QUESTION

Why would Jackson's side agree to settle out of court, given his claims of innocence and the questionable evidence against him? His attorneys apparently decided there were many factors that argued against taking the case to civil court. Among them was the fact that Jackson's emotional fragility would be tested by the oppressive media coverage that would likely plague the singer day after day during a trial that could last as long as six months. Politics and racial issues had also seeped into legal proceedings—particularly in Los Angeles, which was still recovering from the Rodney King ordeal—and the defense feared that a court of law could not be counted on to deliver justice. Then, too, there was the jury mix to consider. As one attorney says, "They figured that Hispanics might resent [Jackson] for his money, blacks might resent him for trying to be white, and whites would have trouble getting around the molestation issue." In Resnick's opinion, "The hysteria is so great and the stigma [of child molestation] is so strong, there is no defense against it."

Jackson's lawyers also worried about what might happen if a criminal trial followed, particularly in Santa Barbara, which is a largely white, conservative, middle-to-upper-class community. Any way the defense looked at it, a civil trial seemed too big a gamble. By meeting the terms of a civil settlement, sources say, the lawyers figured they could forestall a criminal trial through a tacit understanding that Chandler would agree to make his son unavailable to testify.

Others close to the case say the decision to settle also probably had to do with another factor—the lawyers' reputations. "Can you imagine what would happen to an attorney who lost the Michael Jackson case?" says Anthony Pellicano. "There's no way for all three lawyers to come out winners unless they settle. The only person who lost is Michael Jackson." But Jackson, says Branca, "changed his mind about [taking the case to trial] when he returned to this country. He hadn't seen the massive coverage and how hostile it was. He just wanted the whole thing to go away."

On the other side, relationships among members of the boy's family had become bitter. During a meeting in Larry Feldman's office in late 1993, Chandler, a source says, "completely lost it and beat up Dave [Schwartz]." Schwartz, having separated from June by this time, was getting pushed out of making decisions that affected his stepson, and he resented Chandler for taking the boy and not returning him.

"Dave got mad and told Evan this was all about extortion, anyway, at which point Evan stood up, walked over and started hitting Dave," a second source says.

To anyone who lived in Los Angeles in January 1994, there were two main topics of discussion—the earthquake and the Jackson settlement. On January 25, Jackson agreed to pay the boy an undisclosed sum. The day before, Jackson's attorneys had withdrawn the extortion charges against Chandler and Rothman.

The actual amount of the settlement has never been revealed, although speculation has placed the sum around $15 million. One source says Chandler and June Chandler Schwartz received up to $2 million each, while attorney Feldman might have gotten up to 25 percent in contingency fees. The rest of the money is being held in trust for the boy and will be paid out under the supervision of a court-appointed trustee.

A MATTER OF MONEY

"Remember, this case was always about money," Pellicano says, "and Evan Chandler wound up getting what he wanted." Since Chandler still has custody of his son, sources contend that logically this means the father has access to any money his son gets.

By late May 1994, Chandler finally appeared to be out of dentistry. He'd closed down his Beverly Hills office, citing ongoing harassment from Jackson supporters. Under the terms of the settlement, Chandler is apparently prohibited from writing about the affair, but his brother, Ray Charmatz, was reportedly trying to get a book deal.

In what may turn out to be the never-ending case, this past August, both Barry Rothman and Dave Schwartz (two principal players left out of the settlement) filed civil suits against Jackson. Schwartz maintains that the singer broke up his family. Rothman's lawsuit claims defamation and slander on the part of Jackson, as well as his original defense team—Fields, Pellicano and Weitzman—for the allegations of extortion. "The charge of [extortion]," says Rothman attorney Aitken, "is totally untrue. Mr. Rothman has been held up for public ridicule, was the subject of a criminal investigation and suffered loss of income." (Presumably, some of Rothman's lost income is the hefty fee he would have received had he been able to continue as Chandler's attorney through the settlement phase.)

As for Michael Jackson, "he is getting on with his life," says publicist Michael Levine. Now married, Jackson also recently recorded three new songs for a greatest-hits album and completed a new music video called "History."

And what became of the massive investigation of Jackson? After millions of dollars were spent by prosecutors and police departments in two jurisdictions, and after two grand juries questioned close to 200 witnesses, including 30 children who knew Jackson, not a single corroborating witness could be found. (In June 1994, still determined to find even one corroborating witness, three prosecutors and two police detectives flew to Australia to again question Wade Robson, the boy who had acknowledged that he'd slept in the same bed with Jackson. Once again, the boy said that nothing bad had happened.)

The sole allegations leveled against Jackson, then, remain those made by one youth, and only after the boy had been give a potent hypnotic drug, leaving him susceptible to the power of suggestion.

"I found the case suspicious," says Dr. Underwager, the Minneapolis psychiatrist, "precisely because the only evidence came from one boy. That would be highly unlikely. Actual pedophiles have an average of 240 victims in their lifetime. It's a progressive disorder. They're never satisfied."

Given the slim evidence against Jackson, it seems unlikely he would have been found guilty had the case gone to trial. But in the court of public opinion, there are no restrictions. People are free to speculate as they wish, and Jackson's eccentricity leaves him vulnerable to the likelihood that the public has assumed the worst about him.

So is it possible that Jackson committed no crime—that he is what he has always purported to be, a protector and not a molester of children? Attorney Michael Freeman thinks so: "It's my feeling that Jackson did nothing wrong and these people [Chandler and Rothman] saw an opportunity and programmed it. I believe it was all about money."

To some observers, the Michael Jackson story illustrates the dangerous power of accusation, against which there is often no defense—particularly when the accusations involve child sexual abuse. To others, something else is clear now—that police and prosecutors spent millions of dollars to create a case whose foundation never existed.

—GQ October 1994.
Copyright© by Mary A. Fischer 2003

Michael Jackson, King of Pop. 1958-2009

14128829R00026

Made in the USA
San Bernardino, CA
16 August 2014